Gingerbread

RECIPE FOR GINGERBREAD

- half cup of butter
- half cup of sugar
- one cup of molasses
- two cups of flour
- one tablespoon of ginger
- one teaspoon of baking soda

Eleanor Sinclair

Mom and I are going to make gingerbread.

We need all of these things.

I measure a **half cup** of butter.

We measure a **half cup** of sugar.

We measure **one cup** of molasses.

Mom melts the butter in a saucepan.
She adds the molasses and sugar.

I use a whisk to beat two eggs.
Then Mom adds the eggs to the saucepan.

I measure **two cups** of flour.
I measure **one tablespoon** of ginger.
I measure **one teaspoon** of baking soda.

Mom adds the butter, molasses,
and sugar to the mixing bowl.

Mom uses butter to grease a baking pan.

Mom pours the mixture into the baking pan.

We bake the gingerbread for
30 minutes.

We decorate the gingerbread.
We cut the gingerbread into squares.

Now the gingerbread is ready to eat.
Yum!

Picture Glossary

 baking pan

 bowl

 measuring cup

 saucepan

tablespoon

teaspoon

 whisk